WE SAID YES THEN
AND WE SAY YES NOW...

love
don't
CHANGE

BY FRANKLIN & SABRINA WESTMORELAND

Because There's More Publishing | Georgia

Unless otherwise noted, scripture quotations are taken from the King James Version and New King James Version of the Holy Bible.

ISBN: 979-8-9921977-8-5 (Hardback)
ISBN: 979-8-9921977-9-2 (Paperback)

Printed in the United States of America.

Published by:
Because There's More Publishing LLC
PO Box 390163
Snellville, GA 30039
becausetheresmorepublishing.com

REVIEWS

"I recently read a quote about life that included this line: "Marriage is hard; divorce is hard. Choose your hard." In their book, *Love Don't Change*, the Westmorelands instruct us so beautifully about the many ways we can CHOOSE to make our marriages not only survive but THRIVE in today's world!

When we make a conscious decision to truly live the vows we make, not only to our spouses, but to God Himself when we become married, we will discover what true marital bliss really is! The honeymoon never has to be over if you will simply open yourself up to the messages in the "Westmoreland Chronicles."

Whether you are single and searching for your soul mate, happily married, or struggling for your marriage to survive, I believe *Love Don't Change* will provide you with a handbook that will benefit you for years to come, so you too can #Liveyourdream!"

- Dr. Chris Bowen

"I've known the Westmorelands for more than a decade, and their love and commitment for each other is just as strong, if not stronger than the day they initially exchanged their vows and said, "I do." *Love Don't Change* is your front-row seat into the wonders of marriage with the Westmorelands taking center stage. Their transparency, wisdom, and insightfulness shared throughout this book is refreshing. You will smile, pause to reflect, and experience your own aha moments as you peruse this work. As a single woman with a desire to be married, their marriage gives me hope that one day soon, I too will have my own story of how *Love Don't Change*."

- Lanetta Allen

"When I think of the internal working components of marriage which some being: love, commitment, forgiveness, faithfulness, endurance, and support, I automatically think of the Westmorelands. For the time that my husband and I have had the privilege of being connected to them, we have been eyewitnesses of these components at work in their marriage. It brings sincere joy to know that what God has allowed them to experience together during their marriage has manifested into this dynamic work that will change the lives of those who are married, separated, contemplating divorce, as well as those who are single and desire to one day be united in holy matrimony. The stories shared, the wisdom imparted, as well as the practical activities presented in this well-orchestrated work will prove effective in your life if you learn from them, apply them, and trust God to do the rest. We are so grateful to know and have Pastors Franklin and Sabrina Westmoreland in our lives and to serve as examples of God's ordained will for marriage."

- Pastor Michelle Johnson

DEDICATION

We dedicate this book to our parents:
Charlie & Osie Westmoreland and
Clarence & Glenys Simmons.
Through their example, we learned
the power of love,
the power of respect,
the power of forgiveness,
and the ability to build much with little.
Their resiliency in the most challenging of times
taught us the importance of keeping God first
and maintaining a posture of prayer.
We are forever grateful for
their impartation and legacy.

ACKNOWLEDGMENTS

We must first acknowledge God who is our life. Without Him, there would be no us. We are truly grateful for the many things He's developed and matured us through as a married couple. We are wiser, stronger, and more determined than ever to glorify God with our marriage.

Thank you to our uncle and aunt, Silas & Rosemary Buchanan. Your 35 years of marriage has truly been an inspiration to us. Your steadfastness and commitment to one another is amazing to behold.

Thank you, Bishop Kent & Pastor Diana Branch, for your leadership, wise counsel, and instruction. We still remember the word you shared with us during our counseling session, *Love Don't Change*. Those words echo in our hearts daily and will always be our marriage motto.

Thank you, Lanetta Allen, for your friendship, prayers, and encouragement. Your love for us has never wavered. You have been with us from the beginning and are truly an example of what having a godly sister and friend is all about.

Thank you, Michelle & Duke Johnson, for your friendship, support, prayers, and genuine heart for

God and His people. Our lives are enriched because of your presence.

Thank you, Dr. Chris Bowen, for your impartation through the Next Level Leadership class. We've learned so much about teamwork, relationships, and more. These sessions have enlightened us, stirred our hearts, and increased our desire for more of God.

FOREWORD

Every marriage is always either growing together or growing apart. That is because it is a relationship and relationships never stand still. If you are not growing closer to your husband or your wife right now, you are growing further apart; little by little. Relationships, especially a marriage between a husband and a wife, never stand still.

Proverbs 24:3 (TEV) says, "Through wisdom a house is built, and by understanding it is established." Paul prays in Philippians 1:9 (NKJV) "And this I pray, that your love may abound still more and more (will keep on growing) in knowledge and all discernment."

Marriages do not automatically grow. It's not like, "I've got you, Babe! Now for the rest of our lives it's just going to keep on growing." No, it takes wisdom, understanding, knowledge and all discernment.

I have said this for years, GOOD MARRIAGES DON'T JUST HAPPEN! Marriages are what you make them. If you put the effort into them and you learn the right understanding and insight, and you learn the knowledge and wisdom it takes to build a great relationship, you can have a fantastic relationship, no matter what it has been up to this date!

Trust me when I tell you that any marriage that looks like heaven has been through hell to get there. Your marriage is either thriving, striving, surviving, or dying. But no matter what stage you find yourselves, you have to choose every day to work at your marriage. It won't happen by accident or default. It will take work (in some seasons lots of it), but if you work at it, your marriage will work!

I believe that many of the principles you will learn in this book written by Pastors Franklin and Sabrina Westmoreland, will help you do just that, it will give you the tools to work at your marriage.

So, as you read through each chapter, take good notes, and have the conversations together. Most importantly, whatever you do, don't sleepwalk through your marriage, tend the fires to keep it alive and strong!

Pastor Chris Daigle
New Covenant
www.wearenewcovenant.org

CONTENTS

CHAPTER 1

The Vow

A Lifetime of Intentional "I Dos"

"Delight yourself also in the Lord, and He shall give you the desires of your heart." - Psalm 37:4

This scripture resonates with us on so many levels. As singles, we both prayed and believed God for a spouse. We each had our list of must-haves related to our future mate's relationship with God, character traits, physical appearance, and other qualities we considered important. Having experienced divorce, we were determined that this time would be different. We wanted the kind of marriage where the two truly become one. A marriage that glorifies God, with a foundation built on love, His Word, and prayer. We can honestly say that God gave us the desires of our hearts, although not in the way we had imagined.

Sabrina and I attended the same church and would see each other occasionally, but no sparks were flying. It wasn't until we signed up for the same Bible class that we really began to interact - and even then, it was mostly about the Word. We started off as study buddies. Then, the relationship blossomed into a thriving friendship, which eventually grew into a courtship and, in 2010, a marriage.

God gave us a new beginning - a fresh start. On March 27, 2010, we vowed to have and to hold from that day forward, for better, for worse, for richer, for poorer, in sickness and in health, to love and to cherish, until we were parted by death. This was our solemn vow.

As we stood before God, family, and friends, we spoke our vows with the full understanding that with God, we could conquer anything that came our way. We purposed in our hearts not to allow anything or anyone to come between us. Our wedding day was the beginning of a lifetime of intentional "I dos."

Now, as a married couple, we intentionally live out our vows every day. It's a daily choice. Sabrina and I choose to prioritize our relationship with God and with each other. We are intentional in our love. We are intentional in our communication. We are intentional in how we serve and care for one another. We are intentional about our date nights and getaways. We are intentional about covering our marriage and each other in prayer, and so much more.

> **IN·TEN·TION·AL·I·TY**
> *The fact of being deliberate or purposive.*
> Google Dictionary

Becoming one and maintaining our vows doesn't happen by accident. It requires intentionality. We must be deliberate and purposeful in upholding our vows because marriage, with all its beauty and rewards, isn't always a bed of roses. You will experience challenges, disagreements (or what we like to call "heated fellowships"), and even moments when you question whether you married the right person. The impact of those moments on the overall health of your marriage is determined by how you respond. Remember your vows when you respond.

It's also important to remember that a godly marriage has an adversary who is always lurking, waiting for an opportunity to cause disruption. It's our responsibility to stay alert to his schemes and deny him access. Be intentional about protecting your marriage and maintaining the promises you made - your solemn vow to one another.

Here are just a few areas where intentionality is key for married couples:

- Pray and meditate on God's Word together.
- Learn one another and grow together.
- Love in action.
- Respect, honor, and value one another.

- Work as a team.
- Communicate always and about everything.
- Spend quality time and have fun together.
- Provide emotional support to one another.
- Manage stress before it manages you.

Our Covenant Commitment

With God at the center, we choose to walk in love, to serve with humility, and to protect the sacred bond we share. We will be intentional in our words, in our actions, and in our prayers. Today, and every day, we reaffirm our vow: to love, to honor, and to cherish.

Moment of Reflection:

Reflect on the vows you made to one another on your wedding day. Are there any vows that need to be renewed? Are there new vows you desire to make to one another today? What steps can you take, starting today, to live out your vows with greater intentionality?

_____

_____

CHAPTER 2

Grace for the Assignment

Becoming one...

"Therefore a man shall leave his father and his mother and be joined to his wife, and they shall become one flesh." – Genesis 2:24

Marriage is work, not in a negative sense. We simply mean that it requires mental and physical exertion from both spouses. It will demand your commitment, engagement, sacrifice, and more to realize its full potential and blossom into all that God purposed. That's why it is so important to acknowledge and seek God both before and after saying "I do." You want to make sure you're being led by the Spirit in the joining and in your becoming one. When you say "I do," it's not just to your spouse, but to God's purpose and destiny for your spouse and your union.

Marriage is a lifelong ministry, and becoming one is a continual process that God graces us for. In His infinite wisdom, God understood that becoming one would require grace to:

- make necessary adjustments
- blend households, personalities, values, and preferences
- complement ministry gifts
- give each other room to grow

- walk out the purpose for which He joined us, and more

One of the things we had to do as a couple was humble ourselves and submit our marriage to God. We needed His wisdom and guidance for our union. We understood that we could not become one without Him.

At some point in your marriage, your commitment to one another and the vows you made will be tested. Your spouse will not always do or say the right thing, nor will everything go as planned. In those moments, allow grace and love to cover. Missing the mark doesn't give you a license to walk away from your assignment. The same grace and mercy that God has extended to you for your growth and development, extend it to your spouse. Marriage is just as new to your spouse as it is to you.

"And we know that all things work together for good to those who love God, to those who are the called according to His purpose." – Romans 8:28

As we reflect on all the things that God has brought us through and grown us through, we can truly say it has all worked together for our good. We learned how to:

- Earnestly pray for one another
- Talk to one another. There were moments when we had to pray and ask God to season the words that came out of our mouths with love.
- Forgive quickly and love freely, so that bitterness would not find a place to take root in our hearts.
- Be transparent with one another and not keep secrets.
- Extend mercy and grace to one another.
- Build up one another in the areas where we were weak.
- Resolve conflict with humility and God's Word, quickly.
- Become one and are still becoming.

We came to the realization that we are better together and that we are called to advance God's Kingdom and fulfill His purpose as a team.

Through it all, God has been faithful and liberal in His love for us. We are here, sharing our story with you today, only because of His grace. As you endeavor to honor your marriage, know that God is with you and has given you and your spouse power and grace for your assignment too.

A Marriage Rooted in Grace

By God's grace, we are becoming one daily, intentionally, and faithfully. We embrace His purpose for our marriage, trusting that every challenge and every victory is working together for our good and His glory.

Moment of Reflection:

In what areas can you extend more grace to one another? How is your becoming? How have you grown together?

_____

_____

_____

_____

_____

_____

_____

_____

CHAPTER 3

Watchman

ON THE WALL

The Man | The Husband |The Watchman

"Then He spoke a parable to them, that men always ought to pray and not lose heart." – Luke 18:1

When I married Sabrina, God showed me in a vision that I had to watch and pray. As the husband, I am the watchman for my house. Although my wife is a praying woman, prayer must be a priority for me too. As men, we cannot leave the praying to our wives. We must cover our wives and families as well. Moreover, we have got to get in and stay in the game.

Now, brothers, let me talk to you in a language that most of us understand: football. Normally, we can debate about which team is going to win, who has the best defense, or who has the best offense. But the role of the quarterback is generally not up for discussion. Most of us will agree that the quarterback plays a major role in the team's win or loss of a game. He must watch the field, look for openings, and be mindful of timing. He must know when to throw the ball, when to hold onto the ball and run, all while listening to the coach for the next play. He must also avoid throwing interceptions and getting sacked by the opposing team. The weight of the win is on his shoulders, and he can't afford to fumble.

As godly husbands, we're the quarterback of the team, Jesus is our coach, and the Bible is our playbook. We must watch and follow God's instructions as we cover our marriages, families, and households in prayer. We have to be present in our marriages. We must be attentive to our families and alert to what's happening in our households. As watchmen, we have the power to ward off and cancel the assignment of the enemy before it reaches our doorsteps. We have power with God, my brothers!

The Book of Nehemiah gives us another picture of the role of the watchman. Here we see the rebuilding of the walls of Jerusalem and the establishment of a new, thriving community. The builders faced ridicule and opposition, but the people had a mind to work, and their hearts were on one accord. Our stance must be the same. We must be so determined to build our homes that when the enemy sends opposition or ridicules the work God is doing in our marriage, we continue to build, hold our ground, and remain consistent in prayer.

It is our responsibility to govern our home with God's Word and much prayer. As we do so, God will show us how to provide for, protect, and intercede for our families. He'll raise us up to be visionaries, kings, and priests of our homes. He'll show us how to support and strengthen our families. No good thing will He withhold from us (Psalm 84:11).

Know that God is with you and greater than any enemy of your house, man of God. He will perfect those things that concern you (Psalm 138:8). He will deliver and answer you (Psalm 91). He will show you great and mighty things (Jeremiah 33:3). Believe and receive (Matthew 21:20–22). As we stand with and honor our wives, there's nothing we won't be able to accomplish in the earth for the glory of God. Stay on the wall, watchman.

Charge to the Watchman

I am the watchman over my home. I stand alert, prayerful, and faithful. I follow God's voice, I guard my family, and I lead with love and strength. By God's grace, I will not fumble my assignment. I build, I cover, I conquer through Christ, who strengthens me.

Moment of Reflection:

Are you in the game? How are you doing as a quarterback? How can you become more vigilant as a watchman?

_____

_____

_____

_____

_____

_____

_____

_____

_____

_____

_____

_____

_____

_____

_____

CHAPTER 4

Know Your Husband's Needs

Every wise woman builds her house...

As I reflect on the word know, I see another word staring back at me - now. We have to know every part of our husband, not based on where he was (past), but where he is now (present). According to Google Dictionary, *know* means "to be aware of through observation, inquiry, and information." It also means "to have developed a relationship with someone through meeting and spending time with them; be familiar or friendly with." In essence, we come to know our husbands through relationship, observation, and prayer.

The bedrock of any relationship is quality time and communication. Both are key to understanding our husband's needs. As we spend time together and communicate with one another, we become more intimately acquainted with our husband's needs and desires. And let me say that communication doesn't always have to be verbal. You can learn a lot about your husband through observation.

Google Dictionary defines *observation* as "the action or process of observing something or someone carefully in order to gain information." I've gained valuable intel about my husband's likes and dislikes - what pleases him, what brings him enjoyment - just by observing his mannerisms, reactions, responses, and more.

Another way to come to know your husband is through prayer. Go to God, who created him and knows everything there is to know about him. God has revealed information to me about my husband - how to engage, interact with him, and more. Let me tell you, a lot of frustrating moments can be alleviated by taking things to God in prayer.

There is a delicate balance in knowing which of these methods to apply and when. That requires wisdom and being led by the Spirit of God. Let wisdom build your house. The Holy Spirit has a way of revealing to you what you need to know. Let me give you a few examples from our marriage.

Westmoreland Chronicles 1

There were things that I observed about my husband that helped me to understand where he needed to be built up in confidence and encouraged. Instead of going to him and asking probing questions, I began to intentionally speak life, words of encouragement and affirmation, into those areas. I witnessed my husband grow stronger and gain a newfound confidence as a result.

Westmoreland Chronicles 2

Franklin hasn't always been a communicator. When we first got married, he didn't know how to talk about what he was feeling or going through. This created tension for me because I talked about everything, and his nonverbal actions were getting on my nerves.

One day, we were having a conversation, and I asked Franklin a very important question, but he didn't answer in the time that I thought he should. As soon as I got ready to say something to him, the Holy Spirit convicted me and said loud and clear, "Your husband is a ponderer."

I sat up in my bed and thought about what the Holy Spirit had said. Franklin would think about something before he spoke because he didn't want to say the wrong thing. He wanted the wisdom of God to rule in our home. The Holy Spirit was revealing my husband's heart to me in that moment. I humbled myself and covered my husband with more prayer and fewer words.

As I did so, God blessed our interactions, and we began to dialogue more. Now, he's an awesome communicator, and we're able to talk about everything.

*The heart of her husband trusts in her
[with secure confidence], And he will have no lack
of gain. She comforts, encourages, and does him
good and not evil all the days of her life.*
Proverbs 31:11-12 AMP

When you know your husband's needs, minister to them, so he lacks nothing from you. Be his place of solace, his comfort, his encourager, his cheerleader, his intercessor, his best friend and lover, and the wife that he desires. Trust God for your husband to reciprocate the same. As you both submit to knowing and pleasing one another, watch God release a Kingdom anointing on your marriage that brings glory to Him.

Knowing My Husband
through God's Eyes

By the leading of the Holy Spirit, I know, honor, and cherish my husband. I seek to understand him not just from where he was, but where he is now. Through prayer, wisdom, and love, I minister to his heart, and together we grow in unity, strength, and grace, for the glory of God.

Moment of Reflection:

Do you know your husband's needs? If not, what methods can you apply to find out his needs? How can you continue to minister to or fulfill those needs in his life?

_____

_____

_____

_____

_____

_____

_____

_____

_____

_____

_____

_____

_____

_____

_____

CHAPTER 5

Know Your Wife's Needs

She will respond to your love...

"Husbands, love your wives, just as Christ also loved the church and gave Himself for her." - Ephesians 5:25

As a husband, I am committed to loving my wife just as Christ loved the church and gave Himself for her. Having said that, I must admit that I haven't always understood what that meant. But now I know. I am to love my wife unconditionally, give her grace to be herself and grow, walk in forgiveness, support her emotionally, spiritually, and physically, and, with understanding, minister to her needs.

I had to learn to be a good listener as well as a communicator. Additionally, I had to understand that she needed to feel protected and secure with me. She needed to know that I had her, that she could trust me no matter what. Moreover, I had to learn how to encourage and support her in the things of God and be there to cover her in prayer.

As my wife shared in Chapter 4, I had a problem with communicating. When Sabrina needed me to express myself, I would shut down. As a result, she thought I didn't care, or that what she said didn't matter to me. But that was not the case. Sabrina needed something from me that I didn't know how to give.

However, as we both prayed, I began to open up and communicate more with her. This helped me fulfill her need for communication and emotional support. Now, we have a beautiful relationship and can talk to each other about anything.

Men, give your wives your undivided attention. Inquire, listen to, and respond to her. Study her to learn her. What do you see that she doesn't say? What are her likes and dislikes? What are her desires? What needs do you need to fulfill? Spend quality time with her to get to know her more intimately. Use your words to build and encourage her.

Even something as simple as going shopping with her can meet a need. When I understood this about Sabrina, God helped me patiently walk from store to store and show interest with kind gestures or remarks. Now, we do many things together, and I can truly say we are best friends.

> **"He who finds a [true and faithful] wife**
> **finds a good thing and obtains**
> **favor and approval from the Lord."**
> **– Proverbs 18:22 AMP**

Our wives are a gift from God, and when we intentionally seek to know and please them, they will respond likewise.

A Husband's Commitment

I am a husband after God's heart. I love, honor, and support my wife with grace, understanding, and strength. I listen with intention, speak with wisdom, and serve with humility. As I grow in love, my marriage grows in unity, joy, and favor from the Lord.

Moment of Reflection:

Do you know your wife's needs? If not, what methods can you apply to find out her needs? How can you continue to minister to or fulfill those needs in her life?

_____

_____

_____

_____

CHAPTER 6

Let Thy Kingdom Come

God's Kingdom at work in us...

"Our Father in heaven,
Hallowed be Your name.
Your kingdom come.
Your will be done
On earth as it is in heaven.
Give us this day our daily bread.
And forgive us our debts,
As we forgive our debtors.
And do not lead us into temptation,
But deliver us from the evil one.
For Yours is the kingdom and
the power and the glory forever."
Amen. - Matthew 6:9-13

We understand that the Lord's Prayer is a powerful prayer and serves as guide to show us how to pray. We first recognize who God is in His holiness and that we have access to Him as our Father.

As husband and wife, we want the Kingdom of God to manifest in our hearts, our marriage, our family, our finances, our relationships, our health, and more. We want God to reign and for His will to be established in every area of our lives.

We understand that He is the source of our provision. So, we pray and ask Him for resources, strategy, favor, wisdom, and increase to properly steward all that He has entrusted into our care on the earth.

We ask God for forgiveness in the areas where we've fallen short of His glory, and we ask Him to help us extend that same forgiveness to one another and others. We also ask Him to keep us from temptation - those things that seek to entice us and pull us away from Him and from one another. We ask that He seal us in His love so that nothing can separate us.

We pray for His protection and deliverance from the enemy, who seeks to steal, kill, and destroy.

We recognize His Kingdom and acknowledge the eternal nature of His sovereignty, greatness, power, and glory.

When we allow God's Kingdom to come and reign in our marriages, His presence, love, peace, joy, provision, protection, goodness, mercy, grace, wisdom, favor - and all that we need - abide in abundance.

Let God's Kingdom come in your marriage today.

Kingdom Marriage Declaration

God's Kingdom reigns in our marriage. His presence leads us, His Word grounds us, and His love binds us together in unity and purpose.

Moment of Reflection:

What areas of your marriage do you need God to manifest His Kingdom? Find scriptures related to the need and then write a simple prayer of faith asking God to fulfill the need(s).

_____

_____

_____

_____

_____

_____

_____

_____

CHAPTER 7

Grow Together

Growth that Speaks...

Just a little note of encouragement to married couples: **never stop growing together.**

We are amazed at how much we've grown over the past fifteen years and equally amazed at how much love will cover when God is in it. What we love, and what is so beautiful about our marriage, is that we've grown together. Through a myriad of life experiences, God has blessed us to keep the promise we made to each other - to not allow anything or anyone to come between us.

We have grown in prayer together. We have matriculated in the Word together. We have matured in ministry giftings and built ministries together. We worship and praise God together.

Our marriage is healthy and thriving because we seek God first, submit to Him and to one another, and are intentional in our love and care for each other.

Has it always been easy? No. We've had to endure hardships. But those hard times only served to solidify our love and commitment to one another. We can testify that truly, anything is possible with God. Husbands and wives can grow closer, and marriages can thrive.

Together We Grow

We grow together in love, rooted in God, strengthened by grace, and committed to forever.

Moment of Reflection:

List ways you have grown together as a couple. How has growing together strengthened your marital bond? List any areas where you may be estranged and need to come together. Bring those areas to God in prayer and then work together to tighten your bond in those areas.

_____

_____

_____

_____

_____

_____

_____

CHAPTER 8

The Color of Royalty

The blending of the pink and the blue...

The Blending of the Two

When we think about the color **pink**, it is generally associated with calmness, love, kindness, affection, friendship, compassion, understanding, romance, nurturing, femininity, and womanhood. Pink is beautiful and so are we, my sisters. Many of the attributes associated with the color pink are embodied in women.

Embrace your uniqueness as a woman. God didn't create us to be like our husbands. He has given us a certain grace, style, and manner that is uniquely our own. Embrace your femininity. Own it, and walk in it, my sisters. We are gifts, and when our husbands find us, they obtain favor in the sight of the Lord.

When we consider the color **blue**, it tends to represent freedom, trust, loyalty, responsibility, confidence, security, faith, stability, masculinity, and manhood. Many of the characteristics listed here are personified and valued in men. God designed us differently from women on purpose and for purpose.

Our physique, our strength, the way we process - it all has divine intention. We were created to be protectors, providers, risk-takers, and more.

Brothers, walk in your God-given identity. We are men and we are good.

Now, when pink and blue are perfectly blended, the mixture produces a beautiful hue: **purple**. Purple symbolizes royalty, wealth, oneness, strength, honor, wisdom, bravery, and spirituality. When God joins a man and woman in marriage, He creates something new, incredibly beautiful, and royal.

Royal Unity

Together, we are stronger. In our differences, we find balance. In our unity, we reflect God's purpose. Pink and blue, blended by grace, become something royal - one in love, one in spirit, one in Him.

Moment of Reflection:

In what ways are you different? In what ways are you similar? How has God used your differences and similarities to create something new and beautiful in your marriage?

CHAPTER 9

When Love Speaks

The Power of Intimacy...

The Power of Intimacy

Love is always speaking and one way love speaks is through intimacy. Yes, we're going to talk about this in *Love Don't Change*. Intimacy is an important element that strengthens the bond between husband and wife.

When we say, "I do," "I will," or "Yes" to one another, we are also saying yes to satisfying one another's sexual needs. The Apostle Paul puts it this way in 1 Corinthians 7:3–4 (NLT):

> *"The husband should fulfill his wife's sexual needs, and the wife should fulfill her husband's needs. The wife gives authority over her body to her husband, and the husband gives authority over his body to his wife."*

I love the way **The Message Bible** translates this text:

> *"The marriage bed must be a place of mutuality - the husband seeking to satisfy his wife, the wife seeking to satisfy her husband."*

When we seek to satisfy and fulfill each other's needs, Satan won't be able to tempt us with external enticements (1 Corinthians 7:5–6).

But intimacy goes beyond the physical. It also involves emotional closeness - affecting the heart, the mind, and the body. When we are sexually intimate with our spouses, we should be fully present, emotionally engaged, and deeply connected.

Now for a little spice...

I still remember the words of a dear church mother as she counseled me on what to look for in a husband:

"All work and no play makes Jack a dull boy."

Let me put it this way for the purpose of this chapter:

All work and no play can make a dull marriage.

What we love about our marriage is that we genuinely have fun together, in every way. We enjoy spending time with one another, laughing together, and playing together. This may sound super deep to some, but we actually pray for new and creative ways to please one another.

It is our desire to have a marriage that is vibrant and healthy in every way - including intimacy.

Listen up...

Turn off the worship music.
Come out of your prayer closet.
Put your Bible to the side.
(You can come back to it. God won't be mad at you.
He knows this is necessary for your marriage too.)

Put down the cell phone.
Step away from the computer.
Remove distractions.
Drop the excuses.

Intentionally give your heart, your body, and your full attention to your spouse.

Spice it Up. Talk. Romance. Have Fun.

"Marriage is honorable in all,
and the bed undefiled." - Hebrews13:4

Spice it Up!

Wives, confidence is sexy. Put on your prettiest negligee, your birthday suit and a bow with your favorite heels, or something you know will grab your husband's attention. Offer yourself to him.
Husbands, let her know how beautiful and attractive she is to you with your words and your touch. Shower each other with love.

Talk it Up!

Create an atmosphere of excitement and anticipation with your words, so your spouse can't wait to get home and be with you. Send flirty messages. Compliment each other. Do nice things just because. Speak to each other's love language.

Romance it Up!

Creativity and thoughtfulness go a long way and you don't have to break the bank. Think of romantic ways to express your love. Google ideas. Surprise each other.

Have fun!

Enjoy one another. Create your own games. Break routine. Laugh together - it's a great aphrodisiac.

Don't forget date nights!

Make them a priority. They help keep the sizzle alive. Always aim to please God and your spouse. Always aim to respect and honor one another so that nothing interferes with your love or sexual intimacy.

We pray that every part of your marriage be rekindled, in Jesus' name.

Sacred Intimacy by Design

Our intimacy is sacred,
our love is intentional, and our connection is strengthened by God. We pursue one another with joy, freedom, and faithfulness - honoring our covenant and delighting in each other daily.

Moment of Reflection:

How can you deepen intimacy in your marriage? Are there any areas that feel distant or have grown dull? What steps can you take together to rekindle the fire and strengthen your connection?

_____

_____

_____

_____

_____

_____

_____

_____

_____

_____

_____

_____

_____

_____

_____

_____

CHAPTER 10

Love Is

1 Corinthians 13

The Living Bible

The Preeminence of Love

[1] If I had the gift of being able to speak in other languages without learning them and could speak in every language there is in all of heaven and earth, but didn't love others, I would only be making noise.

[2] If I had the gift of prophecy and knew all about what is going to happen in the future, knew everything about everything, but didn't love others, what good would it do? Even if I had the gift of faith so that I could speak to a mountain and make it move, I would still be worth nothing at all without love.

[3] If I gave everything I have to poor people, and if I were burned alive for preaching the Gospel but didn't love others, it would be of no value whatever.

Love Is

[4] Love is very patient and kind, never jealous or envious, never boastful or proud,

[5] never haughty or selfish or rude. Love does not demand its own way. It is not irritable or touchy. It does not hold grudges and will hardly even notice when others do it wrong.

[6] It is never glad about injustice, but rejoices whenever truth wins out.

[7] If you love someone, you will be loyal to him no matter what the cost. You will always believe in him, always expect the best of him, and always stand your ground in defending him.

Love Goes on Forever

[8] All the special gifts and powers from God will someday come to an end, but love goes on forever. Someday prophecy and speaking in unknown languages and special knowledge - these gifts will disappear.

[9] Now we know so little, even with our special gifts, and the preaching of those most gifted is still so poor.

[10] But when we have been made perfect and complete, then the need for these inadequate special gifts will come to an end, and they will disappear.

[11] It's like this: when I was a child I spoke and thought and reasoned as a child does. But when I became a man my thoughts grew far beyond those of my childhood, and now I have put away the childish things.

[12] In the same way, we can see and understand only a little about God now, as if we were peering at his reflection in a poor mirror; but someday we are going to see him in his completeness, face-to-face. Now all that I know is hazy and blurred, but then I

will see everything clearly, just as clearly as God sees into my heart right now.

[13]There are three things that remain - **faith**, **hope**, and **love** - and the greatest of these is **love**.

The Way of Love

We choose the more excellent way - love.
We will be patient and kind. We will not
envy, boast, or act out of pride.
We will not be easily angered or keep a
record of wrongs. We rejoice in truth,
endure in hope, and walk in faith.
Love will guide our words, shape our
actions, and guard our heart. Above all, we
will love because love never fails.

Moment of Reflection:

The goal is to exemplify God's love in our marriage. How are you growing in love?

_____

_____

_____

_____

CHAPTER 11

Love Don't Change

Love is a gift...

This chapter is written from our hearts to the married, those dating to be married, those contemplating divorce, and the singles still waiting on their spouses.

When we were dating, we vowed to each other that no matter what we went through, we would hold on to the words that were spoken to us and resonated so deeply in our hearts: *Love Don't Change*. We thank God for the gift of love and the ability to freely love one another. We appreciate God for the privilege of doing life and ministry together. It's truly because of Him that we are still happily married today.

We choose to keep Him first, apply His Word, and remain committed to one another. We're grateful and appreciative of one another's time invested and sacrifices made for the good of our marriage. We applaud all the spouses who are putting forth the effort to make their marriages work. We know it's not always easy, but it is more than doable.

When we say *Love Don't Change*, we are simply declaring that no matter what life's challenges bring, we shall remain faithful and undivided in our minds, hearts, and bodies. We have purposed to guard our thoughts and reject any word (seed or suggestion) that's contrary to God's will for our marriage. We intentionally guard our hearts against anything that could cause our love to change toward one another - like unforgiveness, bitterness, or a lack of respect or honor.

Some people just want the glamour of marriage but don't want to endure the process of marriage. Remember, the two becoming one doesn't happen overnight. It's a process. When both of you enter marriage with this understanding, you'll be able to extend grace to one another. You'll be able to endure life's transitions together. You'll be able to confront and overcome challenges together with the help of the Lord. You'll come through on the other side as one: stronger together, solidified in your commitment to one another, and with your own testimony of how *Love Don't Change.*

Testimonies to Encourage

After returning home from our honeymoon, we were challenged in our finances. The IRS filed a wage levy and took Franklin's paycheck. This caused significant hardship, but instead of allowing it to create a rift between us, we joined together in prayer and declared God's Word.

Within 2.5 weeks, we received two refunds from the IRS, along with a letter stating they had made a mistake and taken too much money. The following week, we received another refund check. Eventually, the IRS replaced all the funds taken due to the garnishment.

In addition to financial challenges, Sabrina also faced health challenges. But again, instead of walking away, we joined together in prayer, encouraged one another, stood on the Word of God, and believed Him for her healing.

Through every challenge, our hope has been in the Lord. We realized early on how desperately we needed Him in every area of our lives and marriage. Even through the pandemic, which altered and drastically changed many of our lives, we held on to our love and kept encouraging one another to trust God.

He has truly kept us! Our faith is still intact, and our love for Him and for each other has not waned. Our marriage motto has been and will always be - *Love Don't Change*.

Love That Endures

We are anchored in God's love. We remain faithful through every season, committed through every challenge, and united by a covenant that does not change. Our love endures because God's love never fails.

Moment of Reflection:

Consider your own testimonies and all the things God has blessed you to overcome as a couple. What motto defines your marriage?

_____

_____

_____

_____

_____

_____

_____

_____

_____

_____

_____

_____

CHAPTER 12

Marriage Assignments

Bonding time...

Assignment 1: An Inseparable Bond

Items needed:

- Blue and red play-doh

Instructions:

- Choose your play-doh, i.e., blue or red. You should not have the same color.
- Mix your play-doh until it forms one shape and the colors are completely blended.
- Now try to extract or pull out your color only. You will discover that it is impossible to separate the two when they become one.

Becoming one is both a choice and a process that requires intentionality and commitment. How strong is your bond? Identify areas of your marriage that can be strengthened. What steps can you take - both individually and together - to strengthen those areas?

_____

_____

_____

_____

_____

_____

Assignment 2: It Takes Teamwork

Items needed:

- Water-filled balloon
- Romantic music

Instructions:

- Turn on the music.
- Put the water balloon between you and your spouse and start dancing.
- The goal is to NOT drop the balloon. This will require your focus and teamwork; and hopefully, you'll have some fun in the process.

Marriage is not a solo sport. Both spouses must be in the game and fully engaged for it to flourish the way God intended. How do you work together? How do you play together? In what ways can you become more engaged and work as a team?

_____

_____

_____

_____

_____

_____

Assignment 3: Do You Know Me?

Items needed:

- Paper and Sharpe

Instructions:

Ask each other the following questions and then share your answers.

- Where was I born?
- What's my favorite song or tune?
- What's my favorite dessert?
- What's my favorite food?
- What place/country do I want to visit?
- What's my proudest achievement?
- What's a major pet peeve of mine?
- What chore do I dislike the most?
- What do I find the most irresistible about you?
- Why did I say yes to you then, and continue to say yes to you every day?

Did you know as much as you thought you did? Did something change that used to be true? As we grow and evolve, so will our likes and dislikes, our tastes, our preferences, and more. As married couples, we must be attentive, deliberate in our communication, and willing to participate in (or have an awareness of) the things that bring our spouse enjoyment. In short, we must stay abreast of the developments in each other's lives. The objective is to continue to grow together.

_____

_____

_____

_____

_____

_____

_____

_____

_____

_____

_____

_____

_____

_____

_____

_____

_____

Assignment 4: Do You Know My Family?

Items needed:

- Paper and Sharpe

Instructions:

Ask each other the following questions and then share your answers.

- What's my parents' name?
- Which relative am I the closest too?
- What are some of our family traditions?
- What were some of my struggles growing up?
- What's one of my fondest memories as a child?
- Four to five other questions of your choice.

Did you know as much as you thought you did? Use this time to learn more about each other's families. This is also a great time to identify areas in need of prayer and healing.

_____

_____

_____

_____

_____

Assignment 5: No Time Like the Present

Items needed:

- Willing hearts

Instructions:

Think of something that you're NOT doing for each other or together and agree to start doing it today. Some examples include praying for each other, taking weekend getaways without the kids, etc.

_____

_____

_____

_____

_____

_____

_____

_____

_____

_____

_____

CHAPTER 13

Marriage

Decrees

Speak Life to Your Marriage...

Take a few minutes each day to speak these decrees aloud together as husband and wife. Declare them over your marriage with faith, unity, and expectation. Let your words shape your atmosphere and strengthen your bond. The power of life and death are in the tongue (Proverbs 18:21). Choose to speak life into your marriage!

Our Foundation in God

- We honor God in our marriage.
- We are glory carriers.
- We are filled with the Holy Spirit.
- We are the called of the Lord.
- We walk in the wisdom of God.
- We are anointed for our assignment.
- We are walking in our divine purpose.
- We are kingdom builders.
- We are dreamers and visionaries.

Our Unity and Love

- We are one.
- Our love for each other is unshakable.
- Our love speaks volumes.
- We forgive quickly and love freely.
- We are rooted and grounded in love.
- We pursue peace with each other daily.
- We speak life over our marriage and family.

- We protect the unity of our covenant.
- We are intentional in our love and communication.
- We are faithful to one another in thought, word, and deed.

Our Strength and Victory

- We conquer every challenge together.
- We fight for our marriage with faith, not fear.
- We are strengthened by grace and fueled by purpose.
- We celebrate each other's growth and victories.
- We are covered by the Blood of Jesus.
- We are examples of Christ's love in the earth.

Our Home and Family

- Our home is a sanctuary of peace and joy.
- Our family's love is strong.
- We are better together.
- We are good stewards.
- We steward our love, our gifts, and our time wisely.

Our Prosperity and Blessing

- We are debt-free.
- We are walking in our wealthy place.
- We are more than conquerors.

- We are the head and not the tail.
- We are above only and never beneath.
- Health and wisdom are our portion.
- God's Word is our portion.
- Prayer is our portion.
- Peace is our portion.
- Love is our portion.
- Joy is our portion.

Our Individual Blessings

- My husband is the king of our home.
- My wife is a Proverbs 31 woman.

Our Legacy and Testimony

- Our love story brings glory to God.
- Our love grows stronger through every season.
- Love leads us, faith sustains us, and grace covers us.
- *Love Don't Change!*

Father, we thank You for the gift of our marriage.
As we speak life over one another, seal these
words in our hearts. Help us to walk in unity, love,
and purpose - bringing glory to Your name.
In Jesus' name, Amen.